AF322675

BABE AND BUG
EVERYDAY LIFE

To my girls-may you always keep your sister bond and live life to the fullest. Seeing the world through your eyes is magical. Lots of love to you always

Babe and Bug
EVERYDAY LIFE

Welcome to a day in the life of Babe and Bug! These two sisters may be different, but that's what makes their adventures together so much fun.

In this book, you'll join Babe and Bug as they go through their day—learning, playing, and discovering new things together. You'll see how they handle challenges, share laughs, and prove that being different is something to celebrate. So get ready for a day full of fun, facts, and a lot of sisterly love. Because when Babe and Bug team up, every day is an adventure!

BABE IS A BRIGHT AND CURIOUS 5-YEAR-OLD GIRL WHO LOVES LEARNING NEW THINGS. SHE HAS AN INCREDIBLE MEMORY AND CAN TELL YOU ALL SORTS OF AMAZING FACTS ABOUT SEA CREATURES, STARS, AND EVERYTHING IN BETWEEN. SOMETIMES, BABE GETS OVERWHELMED BY LOUD NOISES OR BUSY THINGS, BUT THAT'S JUST PART OF WHAT MAKES HER SO SPECIAL.

HER LITTLE
SISTER, BUG, IS 3
YEARS OLD AND
BRINGS JOY TO
EVERY ROOM
WITH HER
SINGING AND
PLAYFUL SPIRIT.
SHE'S SILLY, FUN,
AND LOVES
CHOCOLATE AND
ANIMALS.

THOUGH
DIFFERENT IN
MANY WAYS,
TOGETHER THEY
MAKE THE
PERFECT TEAM.

BABE IS VERY TALL AND PINK IS HER FAVORITE COLOR. SHE ALSO LOVES ART AND TO DO SCIENCE EXPERIMENTS.

BUG IS SMALLER, LOVES BLUE
AND PURPLE, AND IS ALWAYS
READY FOR A DANCE PARTY.
SHE MAKES EVERYDAY
HAPPIER WITH HER BIG SMILE
AND HEART OF GOLD.

EVERY MORNING STARTS WITH A ROUTINE TO SET THEM UP FOR A FUN FILLED DAY. BABE IS BUSY BRUSHING HER HAIR AND GETTING HER OUTFIT JUST RIGHT, WHILE BUG SINGS A CHEERFUL TUNE THAT BRIGHTENS THE ROOM.

AND THEN IT'S TIME TO PLAN THE DAY. BABE LIKES TO HAVE A PLAN AND A SCHEDULE. BUG JUST LIKES TO GO GO GO BUT WANTS TO BE A PART OF THE PLANNING TOO.

BABE & BUG LOVE TO HELP IN THE KITCHEN.
TODAY THEY'RE MAKING BREAKFAST. BABE IS
FLIPPING PANCAKES AND BUG PREPS THE BATTER
USING THEIR FAMILYS' SECRET INGREDIENT.

BUG POURS THE JUICE WHILE BABE DIGS IN ENJOYING THEIR PANCAKES. "DID YOU KNOW THAT PANCAKES WERE FIRST MADE BY ANCIENT GREEKS?" BABE ASKS.
GIGGLING AS SHE STACKS HER PANCAKES, BUG REPLIES, "THAT'S AWESOME, BABE! LOOK THE STICKY GREEK PANCAKE TOWER!"

AFTER BREAKFAST, THE BACKYARD IS A WORLD OF ADVENTURES. BABE IS FASCINATED BY THE TINY DETAILS HER MAGNIFYING GLASS REVEALS AS IF IT'S A HIDDEN WORLD.
"LOOK, BUG! DID YOU KNOW BUTTERFLIES TASTE WITH THEIR FEET?" BABE SHARES EXCITEDLY. BUT BUG IS ALREADY SPINNING IN CIRCLES, FOLLOWING A FLUTTERING BUTTERFLY IN THE OPPOSITE DIRECTION.

IT'S BUGS TURN TO CHOOSE AN ACTIVITY. SHE LOVES THE SQUISHY MUD AND MAKING A SPLASHING, SQUISHING, SMEARING MESS.

BABE IS UNSURE AT FIRST BUT BUG SHOWS HER HOW FUN IT CAN BE.

IT'S DRESS-UP TIME IN BABE AND BUG'S WORLD! THE GIRLS LOVE TO DIVE INTO THEIR BIG BOX OF COSTUMES AND BECOME WHOEVER THEY WANT TO BE FOR THE DAY. BABE GOES THROUGH MANY OUTFITS BEFORE

...

SHE PICKS OUT A SHINY ASTRONAUT HELMET AND A SILVER CAPE. "I'M GOING TO EXPLORE SPACE TODAY!" SHE DECLARES, HER EYES SPARKLING WITH EXCITEMENT. "DID YOU KNOW THAT ASTRONAUTS FLOAT IN SPACE BECAUSE THERE'S NO GRAVITY?"

BUG RUMMAGES THROUGH THE BOX AND PULLS OUT MANY COSTUMES TOO BEFORE PUTTING ON A SPACESUIT. "I'M GOING TO BE AN ASTRONAUT TOO!" SHE ANNOUNCES, SPINNING AROUND IN HER NEW OUTFIT. "AND MY SPACESHIP WILL HAVE A DANCE FLOOR!"

THE GIRLS LAUGH AS THEY MIX AND MATCH
THEIR COSTUMES, CREATING NEW CHARACTERS
AND STORIES.

SOMETIMES BABE GETS FRUSTRATED WHEN THINGS DON'T GO HER WAY OR WHEN SHES NOT READY TO STOP PLAYING. SHE GETS ANGRY AND HER EMOTIONS EXPLODE! IT HAPPENS SO QUICK AND SHE DOESN'T KNOW HOW TO STOP IT.

BUG NOTICES HER SISTER'S DISCOMFORT AND BEGINS TO HUM A CALMING TUNE. "HMM-MMM, HMM-MMM, HMM-MMM-MMM, LAAA, DAAAA, HMMM. NAAAA NAAAA..." SLOWLY, THE WORLD QUIETS DOWN, AND BABE CAN MOVE ON TO THE NEXT ACTIVITY.

AFTER, BABE IS STILL A BIT UPSET SO THEY TAKE A SENSORY BREAK. BUG COZIES IN TO READ A BOOK AND BABE USES HER SPECIAL CORNER TO FEEL SAFE, QUIET, AND CALM.

AFTER REST TIME, IT'S TIME FOR SOME CREATIVE ART. BABE IS FOCUSED ON CREATING ART, HER MIND FULL OF FACTS ABOUT MIXING COLORS AND PERFECT TECHNIQUE.

BUG, EVER THE MISCHIEVOUS ONE, 'WHAT IF WE SPLATTERED EVERYTHING WITH GLITTER?"

BABE LAUGHS, "THAT WOULD BE A GLITTER EXPLOSION, BUG!"

AND TOGETHER, THEY CREATE SOMETHING AMAZING.

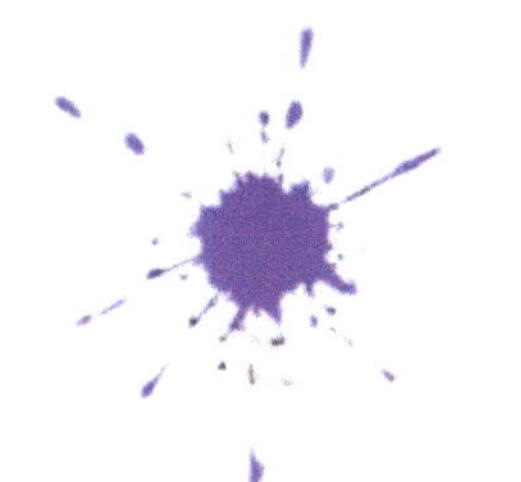

IT'S TRAMPOLINE TIME! BABE AND BUG LOVE FEELING LIKE THEY'RE FLYING, BOUNCING AS HIGH AS THE CLOUDS. BUG GIGGLES AS SHE FEELS A BURST OF EXCITEMENT WITH EVERY LEAP.

"LOOK, BABE! I'M JUMPING LIKE A KANGAROO!" SAYS BUG.

"DID YOU KNOW KANGAROOS CAN JUMP UP TO THREE TIMES THEIR HEIGHT? BUT I THINK YOU'RE JUMPING EVEN HIGHER, BUG!" BABE ADDS.

"WHOA, REALLY? LET'S SEE HOW HIGH WE CAN GO TOGETHER!" SAYS BUG.

AND THEY JUMPED AND JUMPED UNTIL THEY COULDN'T JUMP ANYMORE.

THEN ITS OFF TO THE NEXT ACTIVITY IN THE FRONT YARD. ZOOM! BABE AND BUG RACE THEIR BIKES UP AND DOWN THE DRIVEWAY, PEDALING FASTER AND FASTER.
BABE RIDES SMOOTHLY, HER FOCUS ON SPEED AND WINNING. BUG, ALWAYS THE PLAYFUL ONE, GIGGLES AS SHE SWERVES LEFT AND RIGHT, TRYING TO CATCH UP TO HER SISTER.
"WAIT FOR ME, BABE! I'M THE FASTEST RACER IN THE WHOLE WORLD!" SAYS BUG.
BABE REPLIES, "DID YOU KNOW THE FASTEST BIKE IN THE WORLD CAN GO OVER 100 MILES PER HOUR? WE'LL HAVE TO PEDAL REALLY FAST TO BEAT THAT, BUG!"
"LET'S RACE TO THE END OF THE DRIVEWAY! READY, SET, GO!" SCREAMS BUG.

"HEY! NO FAIR!" CRIES BABE.

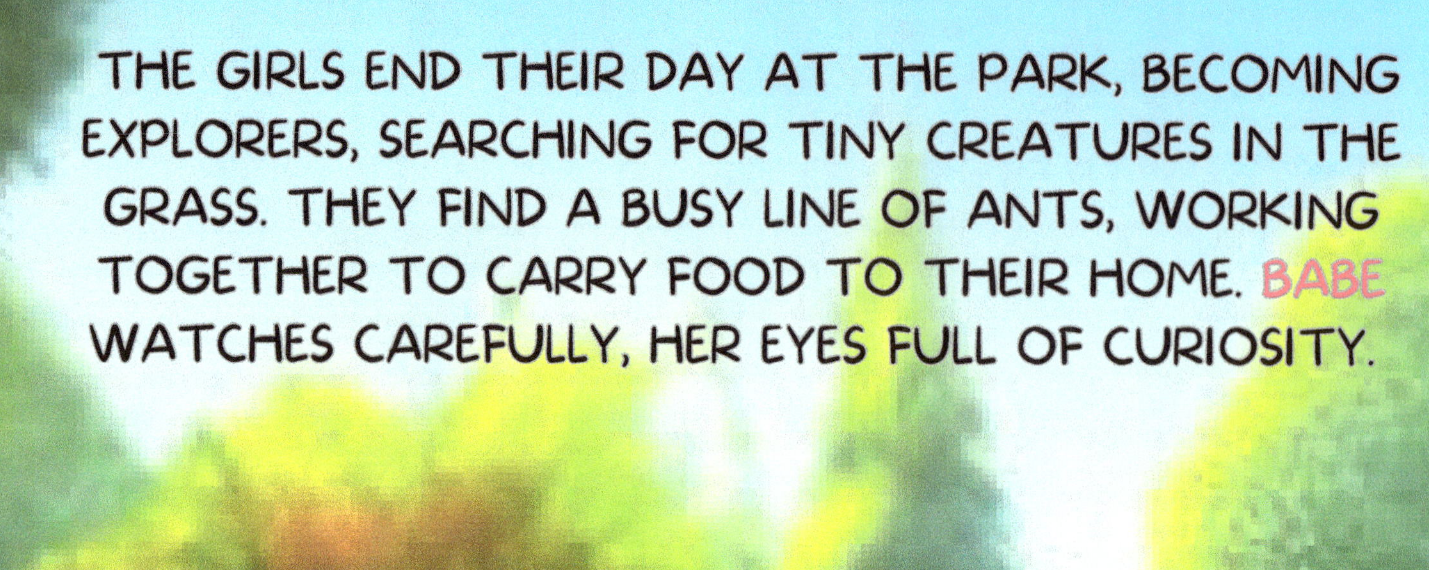

THE GIRLS END THEIR DAY AT THE PARK, BECOMING EXPLORERS, SEARCHING FOR TINY CREATURES IN THE GRASS. THEY FIND A BUSY LINE OF ANTS, WORKING TOGETHER TO CARRY FOOD TO THEIR HOME. BABE WATCHES CAREFULLY, HER EYES FULL OF CURIOSITY.

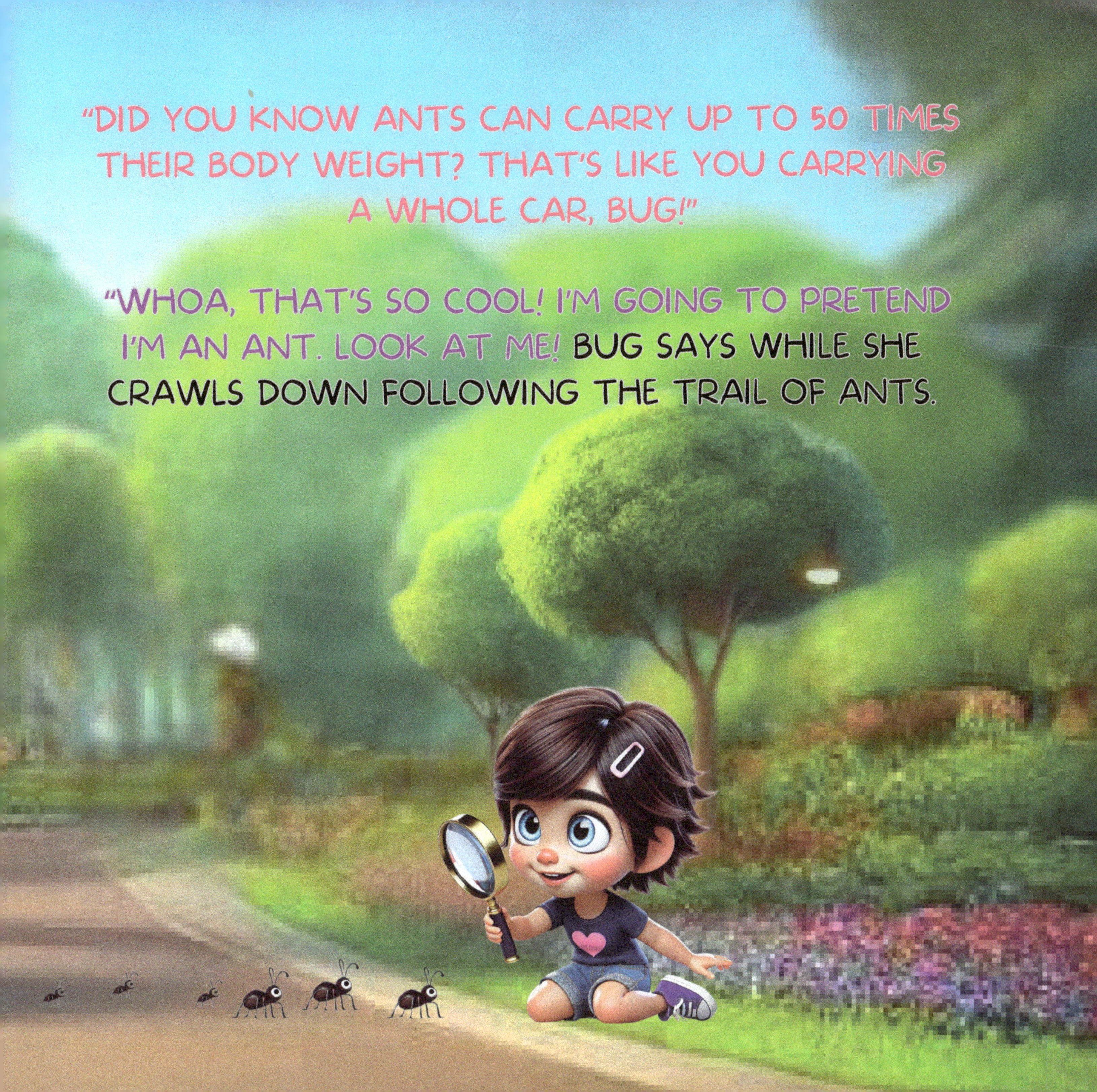

"DID YOU KNOW ANTS CAN CARRY UP TO 50 TIMES THEIR BODY WEIGHT? THAT'S LIKE YOU CARRYING A WHOLE CAR, BUG!"

"WHOA, THAT'S SO COOL! I'M GOING TO PRETEND I'M AN ANT. LOOK AT ME! BUG SAYS WHILE SHE CRAWLS DOWN FOLLOWING THE TRAIL OF ANTS.

AS THE DAY COMES TO A CLOSE, BABE AND BUG UNWIND IN THEIR BEDS, READING AND WATCHING THE SKY TURN COLORS WITH THE SETTING SUN. "DID YOU KNOW THAT THE SUN IS A STAR?" BABE ASKS. "AND SOON THE STARS WILL COME OUT TO SAY GOODNIGHT!" BUG LEANS OVER AND SMILES BIG, "I LOVE HEARING YOUR STORIES, BABE."

IT'S TIME FOR BED, BUT THE BOND BETWEEN BABE AND BUG NEVER RESTS. BABE IS TUCKED IN WITH HER FAVORITE STUFFED ANIMAL, FEELING THE COMFORT OF HER WEIGHTED BLANKET BUG, NOT QUITE READY TO REST YET, SINGS A LULLABY, HER VOICE AS SOFT AS THE NIGHT. "GOODNIGHT, BABE," SHE WHISPERS.
"GOODNIGHT, BUG," BABE REPLIES,
AND THEY FALL ASLEEP DREAMING OF THEIR ADVENTURES FOR DAYS TO COME.

A Note About Neurodiverse Children

Every child sees the world in their own special way, and neurodiverse children like Babe experience life through a lens that is full of wonder, creativity, and magic. They may have unique quirks and needs, but those differences make them who they are— beautiful, vibrant, and full of potential. Embracing their strengths and understanding their challenges helps us all learn to see the world in a new and magical way. Let's celebrate the joys, the triumphs, and even the struggles, as they make our world richer and more colorful.

Helpful Resources for Families:

• Autism Speaks – www.autismspeaks.org
• The National Autistic Society – www.autism.org.uk
• Books: "The Reason I Jump" by Naoki Higashida, "Uniquely Human" by Dr. Barry M. Prizant.
• Apps for Kids: "Calm Counter," "Choiceworks," and "Social Stories Creator"

MEET THE AUTHOR

Marla Godobe is a devoted mom navigating the lively adventures of raising a neurodivergent child with autism and ADHD, alongside a spirited "mini-me" in her youngest. Her children's books capture the essence of her family's unique experiences, blending heart, humor, and valuable life lessons. With a passion for storytelling, Marla shares the quirks and joys of their everyday lives, hoping to inspire and connect with families everywhere.

www.ingramcontent.com/pod-product-compliance
Lightning Source LLC
Chambersburg PA
CBHW040737150726
48196CB00011B/630